To Sophie

Simon Startin

Simon Startin has worked as a professional theatre maker since 1991, initially as an actor, but branched into writing through the Paines Plough 'Wild Lunch' Scheme in 2003. The resulting play *Revolting* was premiered at the Xposure Festival 2003, a dark satire on models of disability, telling the story of Happenstance – 'the cripple that Christ never cured'.

Since then he has struck up a fruitful relationship with the London Bubble Theatre Company, specialising in work for open air promenade. *Blackbirds* is Simon's seventh work for London Bubble and five of his previous works for them were awarded *Time Out* Critics' Choice.

Subsequent work includes: *The Crock of Gold, Metamorphoses, Myths, Rituals* and *Whitegoods, The Dong with a luminous nose, The Odyssey* and *Sirens of Titan.*

Currently, he is on a trainee director placement at the Young Vic Theatre.

For her excellent care of my son Jacob in Year 6

Simon Startin

22nd July 2011

First published in the UK in 2011 by Aurora Metro Publications Ltd
67 Grove Avenue, Twickenham, TW1 4HX
www.aurorametro.com info@aurorametro.com

Blackbirds © 2011 Simon Startin
Cover design © EAK design

With many thanks to: Jeni Calnan, Lesley MacKay, Sumedha Mane, Simon Smith, Neil Gregory, Laurane Marchive, Jack Timney, Thomas Skinner, Jackie Glasgow, Richard Turk.

10 9 8 7 6 5 4 3 2 1

Printed by Good News Digital Books, UK
ISBN: 978-1-906582-29-6

BLACKBIRDS

Inspired by South Londoners,
developed by Jonathan Petherbridge
and written by Simon Startin.

AURORA METRO PRESS

London Bubble would like to thank:

The story tellers: Sheila Bulmer, Eileen Dougan, Daisy Edwards, Betty Grimwood, Len Hatch, Mary Hewett, Sheila McCullough, Jean Muddle, Barbara Robson, Gladys Saunders, Reeny Summers, Brenda Watkinson, David West, Rosie Wheatland, Tom Winter, Alfie Wright and Annie Wright.

The story gatherers: Jasmine Atkinson, George Brown, Sapphire Collins, Louie Douglas, Tabitha Earthrowe-Law, Ella Fogg, Edward Garlick, Merlin Hayward, Billy Hines, Callum Hendrie, Kezia Herzog, Asya Karababa, Geillo Kobba, Suzan Leydesdorff, Danielle Moynihan, Tara Milan-Brophy, Wendy Ndjoli, Daniel Olakolo, Becky Penny, Louise Price, Tommy Pullen, Alex Saoutkin, Karielle Sealey, Tanya Simmons, Amelia Spooner, Jacob Startin and Jodie Witcher.

Volunteers: Mark Bowsher, Gemma Burditt, Sharon Campell, Sarah Cook, Frances Cornford, Rachel Crossley, Pam Douglas, Iris Dove, Matt Dumas Bowden, Justine Earthrowl, Alison Fogg, Elaine Garlick, Edward Garlick, Merlin Haywood, Robert Herzog, Hacer Karababa, Suzan Leydesdorff, Daniel Rands, Sharon Rapaport. Phoebe Theodorou, Su Thomas, Pamela Witcher.

Thanks also to:

Our supporters: The Heritage Lottery Fund, The Arts Council England, Team London Bridge, Rotherhithe Community Council, North Southwark Environment Trust and Hilton in the Community Foundation.

Our community advisory group: Steve Cornish, Dr Patricia Dark, Barry Mason, Carles Ferrer-Miralles, Pam Schweitzer and Sue Timothy.

Our thanks also go to: Gary Magold, the staff at Southwark Local History library and the staff at the Imperial War Museum.

And finally... Sam Steele at Albion Primary, Richard Graham at Tidemill and Peter Cosgrove at St. Joseph's for their valuable advice and feedback on the creation of 'Blackbirds in the Classroom'.

CONTENTS

FOREWORD

Whenever I write I'm aware that the words are only the waves on the surface and it is the tides seething beneath that really deliver. Often these tides spring from one authorial imagination, digging into their sub-concious, sweating over the page and swearing at the pc. Not so with *Blackbirds*. More than any other script I've written, this text is a collaboration of many voices and any authorial services I employed were as a shaper of this collaboration, rather than some mercurial loner preaching truth.

It emerged from a year long project of intergenerational story gathering and improvisation by London Bubble Theatre Company and their resident theatre groups, under the banner 'Grandchildren of the Blitz'. Over 30 local children interviewed around 20 elders who were themselves children during the Blitz of London. The theatre groups, under the auspicies of London Bubble's creative director Jonathan Petherbridge, company director Julia Voce and project co-ordinator Marigold Hughes then explored ways to tell these histories in a theatrical way, set designer Pip Nash researched 'Make do and Mend' aesthetics, elders remembered the details of their lives that even they had forgotten, tea was brewed, cakes were baked and bunting strewn.

This project centred on a a community working together to remember itself. *Blackbirds* is what happens when a child asks an old person, 'What happened?', and a group of people come together with generosity, integrity and commitment to tell that story. The script is designed for an intergenerational community group. There are roles a plenty. The Narration is meant to be shared amongst the performers. There are no entrances or exits; all performers work on stage at all times and the theatre language is that of an ensemble rather than individual star turns. The words of original contributors have been weaved through the piece; their words having more authenticity than anything I could concoct.

The conceit of the piece is the story of what happened to Mayflower Street in Bermondsey and although there is individual characterisation in the piece, it is the beauty of the crowd that predominates. It is a fictional Mayflower Street in terms of the characters and personal narrative, but I hope the spirit of that time is captured. No performer at any time is in 'dead space' but must be busy bringing their own written or imagined characters to life. The more people on stage the better, carrying their lives on their backs as the bombs drop.

In the first month of the Blitz alone 5,730 people were killed, 9,003 seriously injured. In Lewisham about 1,700 homes were destroyed with 23,370 houses seriously damaged. By the end of the Blitz in May 1940, 9 months later, 43,000 people had been killed, half of them in London. The 'Grandchildren of the Blitz' project interviewed some of the survivors of this dreadful time, and hopefully makes fitting tribute to their memories, which are all too easily neglected. In an age when we are connected by global networks, but don't know our neighbours, Blackbirds tells of a time when Britain was at its bravest and bombs fell daily in our streets.

We are indebted to Juliet Gardiner's superbly researched book *The Blitz: The British Under Attack* (2010) for much of the source material in the play, as well as the stories of the 'Grandchildren of the Blitz' story tellers whose patience, courage and kindness have given this project such heart.

Simon Startin

BLACKBIRDS

SIMON STARTIN

A London Bubble Theatre production, which opened on May 9th, 2011.

LONDON BUBBLE CORE STAFF

Mike Adam
Finance Officer

Adam Annand
Associate Director, Creative Learning

Lucy Bradshaw
Administrator

Marigold Hughes
Project Coordinator - Grandchildren of the Blitz

Shipra Ogra
Producer

Jonathan Petherbridge
Creative Director

LONDON BUBBLE BOARD OF DIRECTORS

Pat Abraham, Jonathan Barnes, Haidee Bell, Jocelyn Cunningham, Mark Dunford, Jack Haslam, Simon Hughes MP (Chair), Heather Lilley, June Mitchell, David Slater, Yvonne Stennett, Sue Timothy, Simon Thomson, Francisco Mojica

CREATIVE TEAM

Jonathan Petherbridge
Project Director

Simon Startin
Writer

Julia Voce
Company Director

Pip Nash
Set Designer

Holly White
Costume Designer

Alice Fitzgerald
Costume Supervisor

Myles Stawman
Sound Designer

Alex Stone
Lighting Designer

CAST

Jasmine Atkinson
Lucy Bradshaw
Sapphire Collins
Louie Douglas
Iris Dove
Tabitha Earthrowl-Law
Melissa Erdem
Ella Fogg
Amanda Getrupp
Len Hatch
Chris Hawney
Rosy-Lea Hawney
Kexia Herzog
Robert Herzog
Ryan Hewit
Chris Hiller
Asya Karababa
Hacer Karababa
Ian MacNaughton
Alex Madewell

Rose Mahoney-Moore
Victoria O'Neill
Johanna Petterson
Lee Phillips
Wendy Ponting
Lauren Rowley
Muhammad Salim
Alex Saoutkin
Hasnah Sherifdeen
Tanya Simmons
Faye Smith
Amelia Spooner
Annie Startin
Jacob Startin
Andrew Stern
Maureen Tyson
Patricia Villa
Brenda Watkinson
Jodie Witcher

LONDON BUBBLE THEATRE COMPANY

5 Elephant Lane,
London SE16 4JD
Tel: 020 7237 4434
Fax: 020 7231 2366
admin@londonbubble.org.uk

www.londonbubble.org.uk

www.grandchildrenoftheblitz.com

Registered Charity No: 264 359
VAT Registration No: 240 1591 96
Company Registration No: 1058397

London Bubble Theatre Company are grateful for financial assistance from the Heritage Lottery Fund and the Arts Council of England.

LOTTERY FUNDED

BLACKBIRDS

BLACKBIRDS

Simon Startin

Characters

ELDER	IRIS
YOUNGER	MARTHA
OLD MAN	CHRIS
BOY	FRED
KAM	ALEX
MAY	AMIE
RYAN	LIZA
FAYE	ALEX
ROSI-LEA	TABITHA
ELLA	JACOB
HAM	LEO
KATH	TREBOR
JOANNA	DOLLY
LUCY	ROSE
ANNIE	PATRICIA
EDDIE	MAVE
Cast also play:	FIREMAN
NARRATION	FOREMAN
VOICES	CHILD
SHELTERERS	WOMAN
ADULTS	SOCIAL WORKER
CHILDREN	

*Note: Recordings are used throughout denoted ***

ACT ONE

Present day. All cast on an otherwise empty stage.
Elderly person and Younger person set centre stage to
stand face to face.

ELDER	You're very young.
YOUNGER	You're very old.
ELDER	You make too much noise.
YOUNGER	You're very grumpy.
ELDER	You glow with youth and life.
YOUNGER	Your face is lined and your eyes tell stories.
ELDER	You don't know the half of it.
YOUNGER	I want to know.
ELDER	Do you? Really?
YOUNGER	Tell the stories.
ELDER	And what good are they to you?
YOUNGER	Tell me your life.
ELDER	Before the sun goes down?
YOUNGER	Before the sun goes down.

Tesco's supermarket in Surrey Quays. People shop in the
aisles. An old man takes his grandson to a specific spot.

OLD MAN	Here.
BOY	Tesco's?

OLD MAN	Yes. This very spot. Where that counter is, there was a crane. And I'd be standing here, with my mate, who's dead now.

NARRATION is split between the cast.

NARRATION	We collected stories. About the war and that.
OLD MAN	Stevedores we were.
BOY	I don't know what that means.
NARRATION	And we asked questions. They were children during the Blitz.
OLD MAN	Ships and cranes and crates and boxes from all over the British Empire. It was called Surrey Docks then.
BOY	Why did they change the name?
NARRATION	This is typical.
OLD MAN	I don't know.
NARRATION	And we collected statistics. London 1938. Population 8.6 million. About the war and that. 43,000 civilians... And we found out about this area Bermondsey had over 200 factories employing over... And we found out about a street. Mayflower Street. Population 43. A real street. Round the back of Bubble. And we found out who lived there...

September 1940
Mayflower Street assembles.
Seven different households formed into a street on stage.

No.7

KAM	Number 7.
MAY	The Clarks.
RYAN	I suffer with my nerves.
FAYE	Shall I put the kettle on ?

No.8

ROSI-LEA	Number 8.
ELLA	Blue door.
HAM	Ham Livermore.

No.9

KATH	I lodge here. Number 9.
JOANNA	Sorry about the steam.
KATH	We've got carpets.

No.10

LUCY	10 Mayflower Street.
EDDIE	Mum and Dad's picture's in the hall.
ANNIE	And a funny smell.
EDDIE	This is Nan.

MARTHA	I could tell you a few stories.

No.11 (including Sophie)

IRIS	You can tell number 11 by the pink curtains.
ALEX	I mend radios...
CHRIS	In his shed.
FRED	Nice shed, big.
AMIE	Hello.

No.12

LIZA	The kids... sorry.
ALEX	What!
TABITHA	Don't... no!
LIZA	Stop it!
JACOB	Ahhh!
LEO	Number 12.

No.13

TREBOR	Unlucky 13.
DOLLY	The house is smoky.
ROSE	I love fresh air.
PATRICIA	I love Trebor.

Mayflower Street No. 8 and No. 10
Rosie-Lea and Ella fighting, they bump into Mave.
Martha sitting in a chair, she calls to her grandson, Eddie.

MARTHA	Oi you! Come here and give us a kiss!
MAVE	Mr. Livermore, for the love of all that is holy, you have to get those girls under control.
MARTHA	Won't you give your Gran a kiss?
MAVE	You need to get a stick to them.
HAM	I'm afraid I don't hold with that. Violence is not an answer to problems.
MAVE	Never did my Emily any harm, God rest her soul.

Martha throws out a sixpence to Eddie.

MARTHA	Get us a Guinness!

Jasmine grabs the coin and then runs.

MAVE	Good bit of stick gets the bad out of them.
MARTHA	And don't go pissing off with my tenner!

Cut to Ella and Rosie-Lea fighting and knocking into Mave again.

MAVE	If you can't get 'em fixed I'm gonna be looking for new lodgings.

Girls look worried and stop fighting.

NARRATION	Preparations for war were underway months before its declaration. Gas Masks issued. Municipal plans drawn up.

The people readied.
One of the great fears was a repeat
of the devastation visited on the
people of Guernica during the
Spanish Civil War, when the
German Luftwaffe, on behalf of
the Spanish government innovated
a new tactic: terror bombing.

Mayflower Street No. 11 gathers round the wireless.

RISI	Don't turn it on.
TAM	Come on now, mother.
RISI	If you turn it on it'll happen.
TAM	If we don't know it's happening, doesn't mean...
RISI	That's how my life works, Tam. If you let it happen, it happens.
SOPHIE	What's the matter?
AMIE	There's gonna be a war.
RISI	I've already lost my brother to King and Country in the last one. They ain't having you lot and all.

Sophie turns on the radio.

*CHAMBERLAIN   This morning the British Ambassador
in Berlin handed the German Government a final note...'
*(The recording of Chamberlain quietly carries on under
Kam talking to his children in No. 7.)*
...stating that, unless we heard from them by 11 o'clock that
they were prepared at once to withdraw their troops from
Poland, a state of war would exist between us. I have to tell

you now that no such undertaking has been received, and
that consequently this country is at war with...

KAM   We've something very very serious
to ask you. You are only young
but we have to ask you this very
difficult question. You will know that
many children are going away to live
in the country to be safe, our
question to you is, do you want to
go to the country with the other
children and be safe or do you want
to stay here with your mum and
daddy and almost certainly be killed.

MAY   So. Some kids were evacuated.

Recorded monologue:

*REENY   I was 12 when war was declared and
I was evacuated 2 days before war was declared and I was 12
nyears of age then. And I was taken to Brighton on a train with
all the evacuees. And we was billeted out on different people... It
was an elderly couple then and I was with my cousin and we had
the front room – we were one of the lucky couples you know.
(The children lay out their pyjamas on a bed.)
...They were very nice. But my cousin's Mum came down
after five weeks we'd been there and nothing had happened in
London then and she came to see us on the Sunday and she
went back to my Mum and said 'I think we ought to get'em
home'. *(Children begin to itch.)*...because we'd got louse in our
hair. We didn't know at 12 years of age what it was and she'd
noticed us keep scratching our head so my Mum said, 'Oh, go
and bring 'em back.' So we was only there for 5 weeks.

*BETTY   We arrived there in Crawley, Sussex, a

big hall, I think it was something to do with the town hall or something, a great big room, must have been about two bus loads of children were there and went into this room...

All children form a line and adults inspect them, checking for hygiene, finger nails etc. The boys' muscles are also checked, a few of the potential 'parents' even move up close to sniff them.

*BETTY   ...and saw all the ladies came in, there were a couple of men, they were their husbands, to choose who they were going to take and my mother said I wasn't to be parted from my brother I had to be with him... What happened was you were there all lined up and these women would walk past. Some were a bit snooty look at you, you know you could hear them saying, 'Oh I don't like the look of that,' you know and one lady came straight up to me, said – being fair, my hair was nearly white with a little fringe like that – and the more she kept looking at me and the more embarassed – although I was nearly 7 – I was on the shy side and she just turned around and said, 'I would like this little girl to come with me,' and I said 'But I'm with my brother' and she said, 'For a little while I will take the 2 of you.'

The two children go off with their new 'parent'.

NARRATION   And some kids stayed at home.
                           Where their brothers, and mothers
                           and sisters and fathers volunteered.
                           One and a half million volunteers.

Up on the roof.

FAYE   It's not bad being a watcher,
                  especially in the day.

TREBOR   Sitting up here in the sunshine and
                  smoking and watching the sky and
                  looking down at the people doing
                  their business as usual.

FAYE   Don't really know what I'm watching
                  for.

TREBOR   Don't really know what I'll do if
                  something does happen. Suppose
                  I'll just hike down the steps and
                  tell them that a bomb has just fallen
                  on 'em.

Mayflower Street No. 11.
Tam is reading from a pamphlet.

TAM   'Air raids will only mean a great
                  noise to younger children and
                  provided Daddy and Mummy won't
                  mind, they won't. But it's no good
                  pretending to older children that
                  raids are of no importance. Far
                  better to reassure them by admitting
                  the danger, but stressing the very
                  long odds against them being hit.'

RISI   Perhaps you should have read that
                  before now.

SOPHIE   I feel sick.

Sound of bomber engines.

NARRATION   September 7th, 1940. Black Saturday.

TREBOR   On the skyline, coming up the
                  Thames, black specks like swarms

of flies, weaving their way through
puffs of smoke. A perfect view of
them, flying across the Thames, past
Dagenham and Rainham and
Barking. The docks are going to get it.

Sound of the bombs in distance.

NARRATION   The first bombs fell on the Ford
motor works in Dagenham. Next,
hundreds of fire bombs on Beckton
gasworks. Minutes later, flames
stretched both North and south
of the river from North Woolwich
to Tower Bridge. 200 acres of
timber stacks at Surrey Docks blazed
through the night, destroying 80%
of the largest timber stockpile in
the UK. Thousands of gallons of
burning rum poured into the
Thames at West India Dock. The
whole of the docklands area pounded
with bomb after bomb after bomb.

Voices list the dead.

VOICES   John Addis, Alice Addis, John
Fitzgerald Addis, Emily Beatrice
Badley, William Henry Benneworth,
Terence Alfred Benneworth, Mary
Jane Blakey, Emily Kate Bond,
Ronald Ernest Bond, Robert Edwin
Bond, Pamela Joyce Bond, Charles
Walter Bond, Williams James

Bowden, Charles Mather Brenland.

*A communal air raid shelter. All of Mayflower Street
huddles in the half light. Leo Atkinson dashes in.*

LEO	The docks are alight! The whole bloody world's on fire!
ROSE	Where the hell have you been?
LEO	It's brilliant!
LIZA	You'll get yourself killed.
LEO	Dad said you should always face your fear.
ROSE	Yeah, before he buggered off!

*Risi gets the shakes which the rest of the household try to
calm.*

*DAISY The day of the bombing, like, my
stepmum and I were standing at the door...they started
bombing the docks and then later on, the people who
lived what we called 'downtown', where the docks were,
all came through to go to Keatons Road School...and they
were all killed. Most of them were killed during the night
bombing. That was the start of the bombing.

VOICES	Joseph George Carter, John James Cassidy, Rosina Cassidy, Emma Louise Cannon.
NARRATION	By now Surrey Docks was a square mile of flame. A thousand fire pumps and many thousands of men fought the inferno through the night.

| FIREMAN | I was on the boat patrol. I'd been ordered back to London from a refinery fire at Canvey Island. As we came back up the Thames there was nothing but fire ahead, apparently stretching right across the river and burning on both its banks. We seemed to be entering a tunnel of fire – no break in it anywhere. Burning barges drifted past. For many hours no contact with the shore was possible. We did what we could when we could. |

Shelterers sing 'Don't go down the mine, Dad' by Robert Donnelly and Will Geddes (1910), quiet and tense, comforting themselves.

Darkness. A torch beam passes over the huddled.

| MARTHA | Bloody Hitler! |

Mother and girl pray with their rosary beads.

KATH	I don't think mine is working, Mummy.
JOANNA	Of course it is darling. Just trust in Our Lady. No harm will come.
KATH	It isn't! It isn't working! I'm scared, Mummy!
PATRICIA	Have mine.
KATH	What?

PATRICIA	Mine is working.
KATH	But then you won't be safe.
PATRICIA	I can fix yours. Ever since I was a little girl I could fix the beads. You don't have to worry. Take mine.

Girl takes the beads and woman comforts her.

*EILEEN   It was terrifying, it was really
...terrifying, especially when they bombed the docks it was all alight and erm then we had err... a what they call it... an incendiary bomb come in my mum's bedroom but we was all out in the garden in the shelter but that went out so that was it.

Fierce bombing. Floor shakes. Moments of complete darkness. Then light/strobe light illuminates woman walking very slowly, balancing a shaking cup of tea.

*GLADYS   I can't explain the feeling; there is nothing you can do. You can't run anywhere; you don't run out, you'd just do as you're told.

Bombing subsides.

TREBOR   That night I walked home, picking up news as I could about the East End because we knew it so well, we knew people and places and that this place had been bombed and that, and we sat and had a cup of tea and talked about how people must be suffering, then we went to

bed, with the bombs falling,
wondering if we'd wake up in the
morning.

The All Clear sounds. Light changes.

FAYE	At 5am the 'All Clear' sounded.
TREBOR	A sound like a beautiful symphony.
NARRATION	During the 8 hours of that first air raid: 250 German planes dropped 625 tons of high explosive bombs and at least 800 incendiary bombs, each containing 795 pounds of explosive. 436 people were killed and 1600 seriously injured. 54 were killed from this area.
NARRATION	That was Black Saturday; the first day of the Blitz.

Alfred's song is sung quietly.

ALFRED *(sings)*   We are some of the Bermondsey boys
We are some of the boys,
We know our manners,
We are the tanners
We are respected wherever we go
doors and windows open wide
If you see the copper come,
hit him on the nose and run!
We are the Bermondsey Boys.

Boys play 'weak horses'.

*LEN   We used to play a game called 'Weak
Horses'. Now I've only seen that mentioned once. We used
to call it 'Jimmy... Jimmy Knacker'. You had a boy standing
against the wall, we split into two teams, boy stood against
the wall, the others put their heads and shoulders made like
a horse, the other crew run leap and jump on to you , right?
Then you all had to do is hold them and say 'Jimmy Jimmy
Knacker 123!' but if you collapsed before that we used to
call out 'Weak horses, weak horses!' and you had to do it
again. That was that.

BOY/NARRATION   We learned some of what people
                   went through. Only some of it
                   though. It was in memory,
                   and sometimes they wanted
                   to protect us from those
                   memories because we were children.
                   Sometimes they wanted to protect
                   themselves from the memories.
CHILD   What was sheltering like?

*Shelterers, in a sort of Flannegan and Allen fashion, except
sleepwalking, make their way to shelters, singing 'Underneath
the Arches' softly, with Mary speaking over the top.*

*MARY   We used to have one shelter in the
buildings or we used to have it indoors, but then they built
these two Arches. Stainer Street Arch, they used to just have
to sit on the side of the seats or on that side they used to
have beds, but we used to have one called 61 Arch, which

was a lovely one, after they done built it. They had bunk
beds and people, soldiers, American soldiers used to come
in, you know, see because we used to put our bedding
up every night but in the end, we used to just left it in the
corner for night time... that's where bingo came out of, 61
Arch. And it was all elderly people, and the children, see,
they just wanted to play, but the grown ups used to just play
bingo, although it was called 'Azzie Azzie', back then. You
know, and American soldiers, they used to come in and
fetch in things like chocolate, sweets and that, stockings for
the woman, so we didn't let them get us down.

*The shelter is more ordered now. A child dances watched
by very tired shelterers.*

*BRENDA   We sheltered mostly in the railway
arches, which are still there, on the other side of the road.
The one we used to use was the metal working factory,
sheet metal, cutting metal for industry, and we went there
at night for company and this was heaven to me because I
always wanted to entertain: singing and dancing and being
on the stage was my aim in life. So I pretended that I was in
the theatre. I had no costume of course but it was all in the
mind. I used to go a lot behind all the machinery, pretend
that I was in my dressing room, and then I would come out
and sing and dance to the people who were sheltering and it
cheered them up; and it took their minds off the raid. They
would join in, so you see you couldn't shut me up.

*Shelterers speak the second verse of John Betjeman's 'In
Westminster Abbey'.*

*Mayflower Street No. 13. Trebor sleeps in his chair, still
wearing his ARP uniform.*

PATRICIA   Wake your dad up, it's tea time.
                    (The children don't move.) Wake
                    him up. What's wrong with you?

ROSE   But he shouts.

PATRICIA   Course he shouts. He was up all
                    night. Seeing God knows what. Now
                    do it.

DOLLY *(Holding out her hand to nudge him but doesn't dare.)*
                    Dad. Dad. Dad? *(She touches him.)*

TREBOR   Jesus Christ! No!

*The children scarper. Trebor recovers from his
nightmares.*

TREBOR   Is it tea?

The girls narrate.

NARRATION   The country was divided into 111
                    warning districts
                    How to protect people; that was
                    what exercised civil servants and
                    the government. The country was
                    divided into 111 warning districts.
                    Messages about approaching enemy
                    aircraft from RAF fighter command
                    were cascaded to the control centres
                    via direct telephone lines.

*The boys fly in with a cascade of phones and a tangle of
phone lines.*

NARRATION   The control centres would then pass

the information onto those on a prioritised warning list.
Government offices first then Civil Defence HQ's
Fire brigades
And large factories.
Each stage of the alert was given a colour code name:

FOREMAN *(Shouts)* Yellow!

NARRATION Yellow was 'Preliminary Caution'
Meaning that planes were 22 minutes away

FOREMAN Red!

NARRATION Red was 'Action Warning'.
Planes twelve minutes away.
Air raid sirens activated.
Green is 'All clear'.
Raiders passed.

SHELTERER Anyone heard the green?

ALL No.

NARRATION In July 1940, the government shifted from 'safety first' to 'production first', as air raids were disrupting wartime production and a purple colour code was introduced.
Purple meant the factory was in the flight path, but not expected to be a target.

Mayflower Street No. 8.
Ham is struggling with the instructions for 'How to build an Anderson Shelter', hammers wood and nails strewn about.

ROSIE-LEA   Dad? Ella keeps sticking nails into bunny.

Bunny (toy) is not looking that well. Like a bunny from hellraiser.

ELLA   That's a lie. I was only going to cut her hair and Rosie called me a pig.

ROSIE-LEA   You are a pig.

HAM   Please children, I just need a few moments peace. I'm trying to build us an Anderson shelter, but the instructions don't make any sense.

ELLA   Well, you're a big fat smelly poo from a pig's bum.

ROSIE-LEA   Dad?!

HAM   Please children. A little peace

(Pause.)

ELLA   Poo!

ROSIE-LEA   Pig!

Ham explodes.

HAM   OH FOR GOD'S SAKE WILL YOU SHUT UP! IF I DON'T GET THIS BUILT WE'LL BE DEAD. IS THAT CLEAR? *(Silence.)*

ROSIE-LEA   Dad?

HAM *(Restraining himself)* What is it now?

ROSIE-LEA   You've got the instructions upside down.

*SHEILA   There was a sand bag shelter in the

square where I lived, and a brick shelter and they made
shelters under the flats. We slept down there and I had a top
bunk. My head was there and there was a boy there. I used
to say to my mum, 'Oh, Jimmy Fisher's feet smell!' And she
turned me round. Oh Jimmy Fisher! I was about 8.

NARRATION	Eventually, 2.5 million Anderson shelters were issued to households in large towns. To shelter 10 million of the 27 million potentially at risk.
HAM	Whilst not bomb proof against a direct hit, they were pretty effective against flying debris and blast shock.

*Mayflower Street No. 10. The family is trying to squeeze
Martha into the Anderson Shelter, but she is putting up
a fight.*

MARTHA	I'm not going in that stinking hole.
LUCY	Mind her leg.
MARTHA	I'd rather be blown to pieces.
LUCY	Nearly there now.
EDDIE	She won't fit. Where are we going to go?
ANNIE	She's doing it deliberately.
EDDIE	Couldn't we leave her outside?
MARTHA	Show some respect you little bleeder.

They squeeze her into the shelter.

MARTHA	God, its worse than bleedin' steerage.

LUCY Then you should be used to it then.

MARTHA And where's me Guinness? I can't be stuck 'ere without intoxication.

LUCY Just bloody button it, Mother!

MARTHA Charmed I'm sure.

Silence. Sound of distant bombing. The children are scared. Martha sees this.

MARTHA We'll be alright kiddies. We'll be alright...

*DAISY ...you lived for the day...

Mayflower Street No. 12.

LIZA Have you seen Leo?

*DAISY ...You lived one day at a time.

LIZA He should be back by now. Leo! Leo! I'm gonna swing for him I swear.

CHILD What's it like to be blown up?

The shelterers tell.

SHELTERERS Syrupy and slow
Time twisted tight around our breath.
Where once a teacup now there's dust
Where once a limb; a lack, a space.
The roof has fallen under me.
The floor is shattered on the stairs.

> Perhaps a glimpse, a panicked look,
> Our glances meet, a thwarted gasp
> Then broken up and naked by the blast
> Your sister takes the moment as her last
> And all the rules are gone.
> The rules are gone
> The hearth and home are up the spout
> And picture postcards from Southend
> Are sent into the sky.

Gas masked figures climb through the carnage.

The monologues run alongside the following images:
   ~A child's dead body is cleaned.
   ~A man calls for his wife.
   ~A woman holds a toy and smokes a cigarette.
   ~ARP man unshrouds some bodies and they gasp into life.

*BETTY   ...we were all sitting down, my dad was still in the garden actually, 'cause he used to – although he had a tin hat he never wore it – used to get told off for that – but he'd come home that day. I know it was sort of early in and he'd just shout. To this day I can hear him say it 'This is for us' and...but as luck happened it wasn't for us it was for the house opposite. It hit the house opposite direct but we caught the full blast of the house it just sort of... everything sort of falls in, the windows, everything sort of in a muddle... where there was a table about this high, my mother says 'Dive under the table!' she's dived under the table and I can remember she was knitting me a dress... and all I can remember is seeing her backside stuck under there. Although she was thin she was trying to get under the table knitting and all I could remember, the wool has run you know.

The gas masked figures shroud the bodies.

*BARBARA   We would hear the whistle, as bombs came down. When a bomb exploded, at a distance, it would shake the whole ground, everything would rattle. Things fall off the mantle shelf. If closer, the windows would blow out – the blast creates a ripple of air, powerful, smashes glass and brings ceilings down...

*REENY   ...And about 6 o'clock one morning all the doors came in on us and the little houses that was along the side of it all got blown up and they had to come and get us out of the ground floor flat, you know. I can remember my uncle running round, calling out for my Mum. He got us out – all the doors – I don't know but probably the old chap who let us sleep there didn't ever have his chimney swept and when we come out, we didn't know but my uncle and that was putting their handkerchiefs in our mouths – getting the soot out of my mouth and my Mum's mouth and that, you know.

CHILD   What happened afterwards?

Shelterers queue in the rest centre.

*BRENDA   We were out. We had no home. The government had what they called Rest Centres. Ours was Credon Road School... It was the school hall. We were just taken there with what we stood up in, my mother and I. And we slept on the floor, just on bare boards, for about a week or so. And then the government found us a home, in a home. It was run by the American Air Force, it was funded by them I should say, it was funded by the American Air

Force, and it was in Woking in Surrey... It was so awful, and
the elders, I discovered afterwards, were half-starved.
(Suitcases are quickly packed, moved and unpacked.)
So they were deposited there, and what we did, we came
back and we lived with Grandma for a while; so that's three
different places already.
(Suitcases are more slowly packed, moved and unpacked.)
And we lived in this awful house, well I say awful because it
was very wet, everything was rusty.
*(Suitcases are opened, contents spill out and are dragged
across the floor, then abandoned and people wander
about, not caring where they are going.)*

NARRATION   No. 11 Mayflower Street.

*Stage clear apart from Risi, who is sweeping up the glass
from the floor.*

RISI   I've put my life into this home. 30
                            years of polishing, patching
                            and scrubbing. Near breaking point
                            with the debts of it. Red raw with the
                            work of it. The rows, the tears... I
                            was beautiful as a girl. It's all in my
                            house. I wish they'd bloody blown
                            me up with it.

Shelterers sing 'Do I worry' by The Inkspots.

NARRATION *(over song)* Bombed out families were
                            taken to rest centres, very often
                            with nothing left but the clothes they
                            stood up in, filthy with dust and

dirt and matted blood. Such was the under funding of these rest centres that very often there would only be a few bowls for washing, with no flannels, towels or soap. One East London social worker recalled...

SOCIAL WORKER Dim figures in dejected heaps on unwashed floors in total darkness: harassed, bustling but determinedly cheerful helpers distributing eternal corned beef sandwiches and tea The London County Council panacea for hunger, shock, misery and illness... a clergyman appeared and wandered about aimlessly, and someone played the piano.

An out of tune piano joins the song. Another raid takes place, the people go through the motions of sheltering – exhausted, dust covered.

Leaflets are handed out. Tea and soup is served.

NARRATION Communal feeding centres were set up. By Christmas 1940, 104 of these. Citizens' kitchens were in operation, serving 10,000 meals a day of thick vegetable soup with a cup of tea for adults and milk for children. But central government insisted that the money be found from local rates. Such was the state of affairs that if a family abandoned their bombed home and moved a few streets away to the next

borough they were no longer classed
as ratepayers, but evacuees and the
buck for them passed back
to central government.

HAM *(reading)*   'Remember, fellow Londoners, your
courage, your cheerfulness,
your resolution WILL BRING US
VICTORY.'

KAM   What a load of bloody piffle. All very
well them saying keep cheerful in
their fancy Whitehall palaces. It's
not those Eton toffs that are taking
the brunt. They are laughing along
with the bankers. War is the best
thing that ever 'appened to them.
This is the people's war. This war
is taking place in the kitchen and
the porch.

RISI   Didn't the King get bombed?

WOMAN   Bloody communist.

KAM   What if I am. The people of this
country are waking up to what this
war is about.

WOMAN   You should be ashamed. Bloody
traitor.

KAM   Why you...

WOMAN   Hit a woman would you?

Ham steps in the way.

HAM   This is not the way.

KAM   What are you? Some sort of bloody
conscy?

HAM Yes I am. That's exactly what I am.

Kam hits Ham instead.

MINISTER 1 The government was determined to monitor the nation's morale. Regional Information Officers were required to report daily to Home Intelligence...

MINISTER 2 From conversations in pubs, in the streets, reports were compiled and circulated to the Ministry of Information and other government ministries.

MINISTER 1 Morale was defined as...

MINISTER 2 *(reading)* 'The determination to carry on with the utmost energy, a determination based on the realisation of the facts of life and with a readiness for many minor and some major sacrifices, including if necessary, the sacrifice of life itself.'

MINISTER 1 Very important... morale.

Cross fades with voices reading a list of the dead.

VOICES Harry Richard Marshall, Robert Frederick Marshall, Richard James Martin, Elsie Maud Maynard, Robert Arthur John Maynard, age 5 months, Charles Victor John Miller...

CHILD   But what did children do?

Shelterers turn into children and play war games.

*DAVID   Well, in those days, people were
    oblivious to what their children were doing and it's
    totally amazing, you know, comparing now and then, the
    transformation, nowadays parents won't let children out of
    their sight almost, also, these days they've almost got to the
    stage where the children are walking around with mobile
    phones reporting back what they're doing all the time, but in
    my time, one would disappear and as long as you're back by
    10pm that was all your parents expected.

*Shelterers dance to 'Moonlight Serenade' by Glenn Miller.
There is canoodling in the shadows. Cigarette posers.
Perhaps a child pick-pocketing and getting caught and
given a clip round the ear.*

*EILEEN   When it was a bit quiet we went out
    dancing and there was a Southwark park club, I don't know
    if you know it, but all... all the soldiers used to get in there
    because they were billeted in the park and we used to go over
    there and you know enjoy yourselves and... err... quite nice...

*Ham with his children asleep against him wearing a party
hat.*

HAM   It was the best Christmas I'd ever
                          known. The bombing stopped.
                          Whatever we had was more than

enough. I saved as much paper as I could to make paper chains. One of the kids brought back a Christmas pudding, although I'm worried where they got it from. I don't know why the Germans stopped for Christmas. Or why we stopped. The papers said there had been no agreement. The children fell asleep and I listened to the silent sky.

MARTHA (*singing*) Show me the way to go home, I'm tired and I wanna go to bed, I had a little drink about an hour ago...

LUCY Why don't you sit down Mum? You're embarassing yourself.

MARTHA You can't tell me what to do. I'm a pillar of the community.

ANNIE Bucket of gin more like.

MARTHA You youngsters don't know you're born.

ANNIE 'Ere we go.

MARTHA You think this war stuff is something. Let me tell you it ain't anything.

LUCY Come on, mum. Have a lie down.

MARTHA You ain't suffering like I have suffered. Influenza; that was suffering. The great war; that was suffering. Broke my heart and killed my Frank. He knew how to show a girl a good time. The Boer War...

LUCY You weren't even born then, mother.

MARTHA You don't know how how old I am. Look at my eyes. Look at my eyes.

LUCY Not a lot going on really.

MARTHA It's all in there, daughter. History.

	My history. No-one cares how I've suffered. Just bombs. That's all there is. Bombs and fancy men and carryings on. Don't think I don't see.
LUCY	Have a nap, Mum. *(Martha lays her head on her daughter's shoulder.)*
MARTHA	When I go it all goes. You mark my words. All gone. *(She passes out.)*
ANNIE	Is that it?
LUCY	Yes.
ANNIE	Thank god for that.
NARRATION	It was a kind of delirium. The Christmas silence ended abruptly and carnage commenced again. It all became normal. You got on with it. Business as usual. Only more so.
CHILD	But what was normal ?

'The Teddy Bears Picnic' by Henry Hall And His Orchestra creeps in. While the next three sections play at the same time and the testimony is intercut.

1. Girls paint nylon lines on their legs to imitate stockings. Boys brill-creme their hair and draw Ronald Coleman moustaches on themselves. Girls watch boys watch boys watch girls etc.

 *ALFRED   ...before the war I saw her at fifteen, then after the war I met up with her again. And...err... then the next time I saw her was two years later, then the three of us were going to Wapping, we was all going down for the weekend and they said, 'Oh by the way we have a couple of girls coming,' and I said, 'No, I'm not taking any girls,' and I said, 'No, we aint got room for any girls,'–'Yes we have they can sit on our laps!' – and who was one of the girls? It was her. I hadn't seen her for two years, I recognised her straight away.

The couples match up with varying degrees of success. Meanwhile...

2. Man looking shifty and walking funny.

*SHEILA   My mum used to make great big suet puddings, you filled up on that and there was the black market as well in the war time. If anyone knew anyone who was selling something meat wise 'cos the men worked in the docks, oh the meat, and Jim along the landing got an oxtail which would make a dinner and he had it down his trousers God knows how he walked, I wouldn't know.

3. Boys form a scowling gang. Cigarettes and posturing and argy-bargy.

*DAVID   When we used to go wandering around the parks there was myself and my brother and three or four other boys, so we didn't regard ourselves as a gang, we almost shambled around somehow, had a sort of unspoken communication, we'd say, 'Shall we go here or shall we go there...?' and of course the parents didn't know where you were.

Silence.

A girl on a bike.

*BARBARA　　　　　I've told this story so many times I
　　don't know if it really happened or not. I was returning to
　　school after my baked potato on my bike which didn't have
　　any gears. (I loved my bike, I used to watch the dogfight,
　　the spitfires fighting over Biggin Hill.) I was on my way
　　to school... air raid siren went, I kept on pedalling to get
　　to school and go in the shelter before I could get there,
　　however, a plane swooped down...

The children turn their fire on the girl.

NARRATION　　　　　A sense of community blossomed.
　　There was a rise in the rate of pregnancy. The bombs fell,
　　day after day, week after week, month after month. But
　　men were in uniform and the dance went on...

*The cast sing 'Cruising Down the River' accompanied by
air raid.*

AMIE	What you looking at Mum?
RISI	The blackbirds. Up there. Building the nest on that chimney.
AMIE	But that house is bombed out.
RISI	Council gonna knock it down tomorrow. But them blackbirds don't know about tomorrow, do they? They don't even know they are born. They just look after their family. There's peace with them. No wars or bombs or all the rest of it.
AMIE	We should scare them off. It's not safe.

RISI   No...let them have today. There's a
                         lot more war to come.

*MARY   Let's hope you never have to go
     through what I went through because you can have nice
     things and do what you want, do things that you want to do.

Children play.

*LEN   They used to play 'Tin Can Copper'.
     You had a tin can in the middle, two sticks, once again, two
     sides split up. One side had to bounce the ball to hit the
     tin can, rush the team would go away and hide and hide,
     not particularly hide, and then the team who was opposing
     would have the ball and chase you and throw the ball at you
     so that was when they caught you, start again, quite painful
     sometimes – the ball a bit hard.

The following intercut with the above:

ADULTS   The young had talked to the old.
                         They had asked their questions
                         And the old had passed on what they
                         could,
                         But there were other questions.
                         The questions children didn't know
                         how to ask –
                         How was all this organised?
                         How did you locate your loved ones?
                         How did you find a job when your
                         factory went up in flames?
                         How did you feed your family when
                         your house was rubble?
                         How did people cope with the

psychological trauma?
Was there counselling?
How was information censored?
Were the politicians trusted?
What criminal activity was there?
How did the black market work?
How were conscientious objectors
dealt with?
Were the churches full?
How were resources managed?
Were things fairly shared?
How were houses rebuilt?
Who paid for those houses?
How did the hospitals cope?
How did nurses cope?
How did doctors cope?
How did the dying cope?
How did the mortuaries cope?
How did the burial grounds cope?
Who was brave?
Who was a coward?
Who was both?
What happened to your dreams?

NARRATION   The ending of the Blitz came on
May 10th, 1941. The bombing simply
ceased. The war continued, but the
heavy bombing ceased, until the
Doodlebugs and V2 rockets a few
years later.

*BETTY   I say I'd live it all through again you
know I would do it especially if I'd been older, oh I would
have joined up and I would have had the time of my life.

*ALFIE   It was a better way of living than it is

today, better way of living but there are some good people out there now, we would help anybody decorate anything, knock on the door and there I was. That was the things we used to do, help each other.

VOICES   Charles George Whitworth, Stanley Lionel Williams, May Elizabeth Willoughby and Ronald Wilson. A list of the dead in this area in the first 24 hours of the Blitz.

NARRATION   43,000 people had been killed, half of them in London.

*ROSIE   Well, what I would like to say is that you children of today are so very lucky, so very, very lucky. We didn't have anything, had our old toys and things, and our sliced up Mars Bars but we were happy... It was a hard life, it was a hard child's life but a happy one. I had a mum and dad that loved me and lots of brothers and sisters. That was life.

CHURCHILL   Let us therefore brace ourselves to our duties, and so bear ourselves, that if the British Empire and its Commonwealth last for a thousand years, men will still say, this was their finest hour.

The All Clear sounds.

In the following section, as the houses are described as destroyed, the households exit.

NARRATION   So how did Mayflower Street fare during the Blitz ?

On the 5th September – the second
night of bombing – a bomb landed
on Number 7.
But did not explode.

Two weeks later, on the 20th
September, an incendiary bomb
landed in the canteen of Gillman
and Spencers Wharf – at the end of
the street.
And was extinguished.

On the same night of the 20th
September, a high explosive bomb
landed on Number 11.
The bomb detonated.

The same evening a bomb landed on
Number 13, and detonated.
These two bombs led to Numbers 11,
12 and 13 being demolished.

Three weeks later, on the 18th of
October, at the same Wharf, a
parachute supporting a landmine,
attached itself to the roof and hung
there... for days. It did not explode.

On the 29th November, an
incendiary bomb hit Number 7.
And 5 years later Number 7 was hit
again, on the 29th January, 1944.

Back to present day. Tesco's, Surrey Quays.

OLD MAN	Where did it all go, eh? All a bloody supermarket.
BOY	Come on, Grandad?
OLD MAN	What?
BOY	Mum wants us to get some *Cillit Bang*.
OLD MAN	What's that?
BOY	It's purple.
OLD MAN	Ships and cranes and the whole world in boxes...
BOY	Come on, Grandad. Tell me that stuff later.

Lights down.

The end.

BLACKBIRDS IN THE CLASSROOM

1. A note to teachers

The 'Grandchildren of the Blitz' project began its life in April 2010. With the help of the British Library and the Imperial War Museum, local young people were trained in interview techniques, then went into the homes of the elders of our community and were told stories about another London and a childhood vastly different to their own.

Although many of London's children were evacuated during World War II, a great number stayed behind: 'If we die, we all die together' – their parents firmly told them. Even for those who were sent away, it was often only a matter of weeks before they were collected and brought back to the capital. Evacuation was paradise for some and living hell for others; facing the lethal bombs of the Blitz was often preferable to the discomfort of uncaring and occasionally cruel, foster parents.

Our young interviewees heard these stories from those who were there; those who lived through the only episode of aerial bombing in the history of Britain. These stories are the foundation of *Blackbirds*. We want to spread these stories further and make sure all local young people have access to them and to the living heritage of their community.

It is our hope that these stories will live on in the classrooms of Bermondsey, Rotherhithe and Deptford. In the following pages are some ideas that may help you to do this; we have included some broad pointers of how to use the script in your classroom, as well as some more detailed ideas for lessons. We very much hope it is useful.

London Bubble, 2011

2. The script in your classroom

Starting points to use the script in your classroom

School Production

Blackbirds could possibly be performed as a school production. There are around 30 characters and a flexible number of Narrators. The roles of adults could be played by Y5/Y6 children and the children could be played by younger students in the school. It could also be performed in collaboration with a local secondary school or 6th form college, possibly even involving parents and grandparents.

Unit-by-unit

The action of *Blackbirds* is broken down into units, each of which focuses on one aspect of the Blitz such as 'evacuation' and 'games'. Depending on the focus of the lesson, the class could be split up into smaller groups and rehearse one of these units; taking on the characters and using the dialogue.

Interview extracts

The class could be divided into groups and the teacher could read out extracts from the interviews. The students perform the action of the extract alongside the spoken text. Some of this action is already suggested in the stage directions, for other extracts – this action can be created and formed by the students themselves. Additional interview material is available from:

www.grandchildrenoftheblitz.com

A Mayflower Street House

The class could focus on one particular house on Mayflower Street, thinking about the characters in that house, what their hobbies might be, how old they are etc. The students could then be guided through the script, i.e. through the announcement of war, evacuation, the start of the bombing – and in small groups the children could create still-frames or short improvised scenes about how these characters might react in these different situations.

3. Session plans

The plans outlined in the following pages have been designed to give practical assistance in the teaching of the experiences of local children in World War II. All plans include ideas to extend activities into other areas of learning.

Before embarking on this series of lessons, the students need to have been familiarised with:

i) The basic timeline of events leading up to the outset of the Blitz on the 7th September 1940 and the planned invasion of England by enemy forces.

ii) The geographical significance of Bermondsey, Rotherhithe and Deptford in regard to their proximity to the River Thames and why these areas were specifically targeted by the Luftwaffe.

iii) The major areas of impact on the life in London during this period, i.e. the necessity for rationing, evacuation, sheltering and the frequency of air raids.

From left to right: Louise Price (10) and Ella Fogg (10) interview
Betty Grimwood about her experiences as a child living through
wartime London.

Activity Table 1: Evacuation

Name of Activity	Activity Description
1) Time Machine	i) Students stand in a circle and are told they are going to create a time machine to take them back to WW2. ii) Mime throwing in objects they would not have had during the Blitz (i.e. i-phone, DS, dishwasher). iii) Go round the children and ask each student what they are doing to throw in – then throw it in as a group
2) Objects from WW2	i) Divide students into groups of 4-6. Ask the students to think of objects that existed during WW2, then ask them to make these objects with their bodies ii) Show these back to the group, counting back from 10-0 and asking them to hold still at 0. Ask other students for feedback – what object do you think it is? What do you like? What works?
3) Listening to recording (R1) *Find local map in Appendix	i) Sit down in a circle and listen to the recording (R1). After the recording, teachers encourage students to reflect on what they have heard i.e. what's she like? How old is she? How might she have felt? ii) Distribute copies of the local map and work out where she lived – relate address to school address, ask where she moved to.
4) Pack your bag	i) Ask students to find a space in the room and to imagine they are in their bedroom. ii) Ask what they might take with them if they were being evacuated – discuss what this might be. iii) Play the extract again and ask children to imagine what they are packing in their suitcase, getting ready to be evacuated.
5) Draw Pictures	i) Distribute paper and pens/pencils to the students ii) Ask the students to draw the things that they would like to take with them. iii) Once they have completed their pictures, ask them to show them to each other.
6) Evaluation	i) Ask the students to make a circle. ii) Go round the circle and ask the students to say one word that describes how they felt about the session.

Evacuation: possible extensions

Time Machine

Discuss what happened in World War II. Discuss how the world was then i.e. was there an internet? How did people get their news in that time? Discuss the importance of the radio as a source for information.

Making objects together

Possibilities include steam train, suitcase, gasmask and teddy bear. An alternative is to make an object with the entire group, for instance, an airplane, a forest, an army, a shelter.

Listen to Recording 1

This discussion could be expanded into discussing WW2 and evacuees more generally i.e. what happened to children during the war? Why? Was it safe for them to stay here? Why not? What happened in London? And in the world?

Pack your bags

This activity could be expanded into an improvisation together about saying goodbye or about living with another family. Show these improvisations to each other and discuss.

Pack your bags

This could be developed by building a character; let thechildren choose a character's name, ask them to think about how they feel. Talk them through the process of leaving. Who will they miss? What will they miss?

General extensions:

In addition to these extensions to specific activities, students could also be asked to write diary entries about how they feel, write a letter home or write a poem.

Activity Table 2: Bombing

Name of Activity	Activity Description
1) Intro	i) Explain that the session is about the Bombing of this neighbourhood. Why was our neighbourhood bombed so heavily? What is here?
2) War Declared	i) Students sit in a circle and listen to recording (R2) which is Chamberlain's declaration of war. Reflect on the recording i.e. who is this man on the radio? What is he saying? What do you think this might mean?
3) Response to Declaration	i) Play the recording again and ask students to walk around the room whilst they are listening to the recording – ask them to imagine how they would feel if they heard this for the first time ii) Ask the children to create a still picture of how they feel, counting down from 10-0, at 0 they freeze. Go around and tap students on the shoulder and ask them to use one word only to describe how they feel.
4) Sirens / Air-raids	i) Students sit in a circle and listen to a recording (R3). ii) Reflect on what he is saying i.e. what are rosary beads? Why might he be using them? Why might people lie on the pavement when the siren went off? iii) Play next recording (R4). Reflect. Ask the students to stand up and walk around. Imagine they are going to school, asking them to think about which roads they would cross to get to school. iv) Whilst they are walking, play the siren (R5). Put students into groups of 3/4 and ask them to create a frozen picture of what would happen. v) Ask a group at a time to bring their picture to life so that each group does a short improvised scene. Watch each group and then ask the class to give feedback.
5) Where are you?	i) Distribute local maps to children – ask them what they recognise, where is their school, where do they live? Ask them to look for the houses of Len and Sheila. Can you see where you live? Talk about the areas of bomb damage etc.

Bombing: *notes*

Local history study

A study investigating how an aspect in the local area has changed over a long period of time, or how the locality was affected by a national or local event.

Bombing: possible extensions

Declaration of War

Discuss this in more detail. Why were people so afraid? What was going on? What was happening in the world?

Declaration of War

Try developing the freeze frames into small scenes.

Sirens/Air raids

Extension possible in building characters. Define a name for a character living in the Blitz. What do you do when you are nervous? Or scared? Do you show it? Hide it? What does that look like?

Extension possible like 'hot seating' the characters. Once students have developed a character, ask a student playing their character to sit on a chair in front of the group (arranged in a semi-circle). The student in role is questioned by the group about his or her background, feelings and behaviour.

Where are you?

Having explored the maps of the local area and details of where the interviewees lived, the next step could be to imagine a character living in this area at that that time. The students could build a character (possibly using idea below) and choose a street where this boy/girl may have lived. The teacher could lead a group improvisation, where the students are asked to: get up in the morning, go to school, think about which streets they cross and what they look like, whether it feels safe, how many of their friends have stayed behind in London, what kind of games do they play?

Visits to areas of total destruction
Identify the areas of Total Destruction on the map (if these are unclear, refer to the map on the GOTB website : www.grandchildrenoftheblitz.com and visit these areas to see what is there now.

General extensions

A possible extension is 'Role on wall'. The outline of a body is drawn on a large sheet of paper, which is later stuck onto the wall. This can be done by carefully drawing around one of the participants. After that, you write down around this drawing:

> Who you are (name)
>
> Where you are
>
> Your invented name
>
> How you feel, secrets, dreams
>
> Likes/dislikes, friends, family members (names)

A possible variation is to write known facts around the silhouette, and thoughts and feelings inside. Also, key lines spoken by the character can be added. Role on wall can help to build a character. (See example overleaf.)

BILLY

His house was bombed two days ago - but his family was sheltering and no-one was hurt

"Can I swap my piece of Shrapnel for a bigger one today?"

Billy is eight years old

Tired - didn't get much sleep in the shelter last night

His best friends are Sonny and George

Likes playing in the bombed - out houses

He has one brother and one sister

Activity Table 3: Sheltering

Name of Activity	Activity Description
1) Intro	i) Discuss shelters. Why were people sheltering? Can you imagine what it might have been like?
2) Listening to recording (R6)	ii) Sit down in a circle and listen to the recording (R6). Reflect on recording: can you remember what Mary talked about?
3) Sheltering	i) Divide students into groups of 4-6. Ask the students to think of a name for their shelter ii) Based on what they have heard, ask students to re-create a scene in their shelter. Think of who you are and what you do, together or individually. iii) Replay recording (R6) whilst the students act what happened in their shelter.
3) Listening to recording (R7)	i) Sit down in a circle and listen to the recording (R7) Discuss recording. What did the girl do? Why? What do people do when they want to cheer each other up? ii) Ask the students to go back to their shelter-groups.
4) Make a performance	i) In their groups, students prepare something that they think might entertain their friends. It can be a song, re-telling of jokes, dance etc. Show.
5) Evaluation	i) Ask the children to make a circle ii) Go round the circle, asking the children to say one word that describes how they felt about the session.

Sheltering: possible extensions:

In their shelter groups, the students can make a soundscape, using their voices and/or body percussion of sounds you hear whilst sheltering. These soundscapes can be put under a scene from a group. The volume of the soundscape can be increased by the teacher by raising hand or touch the floor for silence.

Sheltering
The students can make small scenes in their groups, for instance a small conversation in the shelter. Ask them to think of their characters, their relationships etc.

Blackbirds rehearsal photograph: A boy and his grandfather are shopping in Tesco's supermarket in Surrey Quays, when his grandfather starts to recall his own memories of the site of the shop and the docks that once stood there before the bombing of the Blitz.

Left to right: David West and Jacob Startin (10)

4. Appendix

Track List for accompanying CD

R1   Reeny Summer: Evacuation

R2   Chamberlain's Declaration of War

R3   Len Hatch: Bombing

R4   Sheila McCullough : Bombing

R5   Siren

R6   Mary Hewitt: Sheltering

R7   Brenda Watkinson: Sheltering

Blackbirds rehearsal photograph: Children play a game of 'Weak Horses', one of the games that the children played in London during the Blitz

Transcription of recorded extracts

R1: REENY SUMMER: EVACUATION

I was 12 when war was declared and I was evacuated two days before war was declared and I was 12 years of age then. And I was taken to Brighton on a train with all the evacuees. And we was billeted out on different people... It was an elderly couple then and I was with my cousin and we had the front room – we were one of the lucky couples you know.

They were very nice. But my cousin's Mum came down after 5 weeks we'd been there and nothing had happened in London then and she came to see us on the Sunday and she went back to my Mum and said, 'I think we ought to get 'em home,' because we'd got louse in our hair. We didn't know at 12 years of age what it was and she'd noticed us keep scratching our head so my Mum said, 'Oh, go and bring 'em back'. So we was only there for 5 weeks.

R2. CHAMBERLAIN'S DECLARATION OF WAR

This morning the British Ambassador in Berlin handed the German Government a final note stating that, unless we heard from them by 11 o'clock that they were prepared at once to withdraw their troops from Poland, a state of war would exist between us. I have to tell you now that no such undertaking has been received, and that consequently this country is at war with Germany.

R3. LEN HATCH: BOMBING

Bombing, yes bombing. The first Saturday afternoon of the Blitz. I was sitting at the top of the alley where I live or rather the bottom part, there was a stone block, they used to keep because

at the bottom was Reynold's garage and they used to have a horse
and cart and this stone was to stop them bumping into the house
that was there. Me and my grandfather were sitting there when we
see all the planes coming over and we were looking us and all of
a sudden weeeee – we heard the bombs and that was when they
hit the lower road by the tunnel there and several places. And we
dived for shelter that was between by the top of Fulforth Street
where I lived opposite us in between two blocks of flats – that's
where we ran for and that's where I spent the first Saturday night
of the blitz. And that made big impression on me – I shall never
forget that night – not because of the bombing, because basically
I see how frightened people were – there were some families
sitting there with rosaries which was – how can I say – it was –
wound me up, tense, made me tense, cos I'd never seen grown
up people doing that my mum never did it – she was chapel – so
she never had a rosary – so when I see all these people I said
'What they doing, what they doing?'...quiet me down. When we
got out in the morning, on the Sunday morning, I said what was
that they doing? My mum always told me the truth and said that
they was rosaries – they were saying prayers. That as I say was
a big impression on me in that respect. It was really something
I had never experienced. It made a great impression on me,
it still does to this day because sad to say lot of them people
saying rosaries weren't true Christians, they done some bad
things but that's another story.

R4. SHEILA MCCULLOUCH: BOMBING

In the Blitz – well you don't realise all that much when you're
a child obviously because it's the grown-ups who are having to
deal with it, but you always lived with the fact that you might get
bombed – you had a shelter that you built in the garden, halfway
down into the ground. It was called an Anderson shelter and it
was covered with earth – we actually grew tomato plants on top
of it and it was difficult because going to school, if the siren went

that meant that was an air craft raid. If you weren't near a shelter – which had been built by the government – if you weren't near a shelter, the only sensible thing was you heard this siren go and you fell flat on your face as far down as you could get on the pavement. My Mum was taking me to school and that would happen. And she hated it because we had to have coupons to buy clothes during the war and it was very difficult – if you wanted a dress you had to save up your coupons. Stockings – we didn't have tights, they hadn't been invented – but stockings I think they might have been one coupon, I don't really remember. But you know when Mum threw herself down on the floor, ruined her stockings – that was one coupon. And that was pretty dramatic for her because where are her next lot of coupons for stockings coming from? You haven't got any more.

R5. SIRENS
Fire alarms (start and end)

R6. MARY HEWITT: SHELTERING
...we used to have one shelter in the buildings or we used to have it indoors, but then they built these two Arches.

Stainer Street Arch, they used to just have to sit on the side of the seats or on that side they used to have beds, but we used to have one called 61 Arch, which was a lovely one, after they done built it. They had bunk beds and people, soldiers, American soldiers used to come in, you know, see because we used to put our bedding up every night but in the end, we used to just left it in the corner for it was all elderly people, and the children, see, they just wanted to play, but the grown up used to just play bingo, although it was called 'Azzie Azzie', back then. You know, and American Soldiers, they used to come in and fetch in things like chocolate, sweets and that, stocking for the woman, so we didn't let them get us down.

R7. BRENDA WATKINSON: BOMBING

We sheltered mostly in the railway arches, which are still there, on the other side of the road. The one we used to use was the metal working factory, sheet metal, cutting metal for industry and we went there at night for company and this was heaven to me because I always wanted to entertain; singing and dancing and being on the stage was my aim in life. So I pretended that I was in the theatre. I had no costume of course but it was all in the mind. I used to go a lot behind all the machinery, pretend that I was in my dressing room and then I would come out and sing and dance to the people who were sheltering and it cheered them up; and it took their minds off the raid. They would join in; so you see you couldn't shut me up.

Bomb damage maps

BERMONDSEY

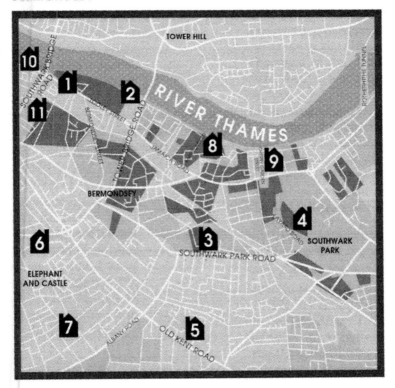

KEY TO INTERVIEWEES

1. **MARY HEWITT** TOOLEY STREET, SE1
2. **REENY SUMMER** TOWER BRIDGE RD, SE1
3. **DAISY EDWARDS** STH'WARK PARK RD, SE1
4. **EILEEN DOUGAN** LAYARD RD, SE16
5. **ROSIE WHEATLAND** OLD KENT ROAD
6. **DAVID WEST** ELEPHANT AND CASTLE

7. **SHEILA MCCULLOCH** FARADAY ST, SE5
8. **ALFIE WRIGHT** FARNCOMBE ST, SE16
9. **ANNIE WRIGHT** CHERRY GARDEN ST, SE16
10. **BARBARA ROBSON** FALCON POINT, SE1
11. **GLADYS SAUNDERS** SOUTHWARK BRIDGE RD

KEY TO BOMB DAMAGE   TOTAL DESTRUCTION   WIDESPREAD DAMAGE

ROTHERHITHE

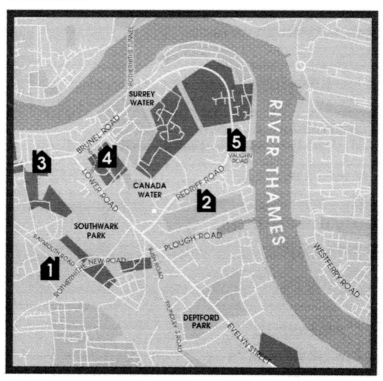

KEY TO INTERVIEWEES

1. **BRENDA WATKINSON** RAYMOUTH ROAD, SE16
2. **TOM WINTER** REDRIFF ESTATE, SE16
3. **LEN HATCH** SEVEN STEP ALLEY, SE16 (NO LONGER EXISTS)
4. **SHEILA BULMER** NEPTUNE STREET, SE16
5. **BETTY GRIMWOOD** VAUGHN STREET, SE16

KEY TO BOMB DAMAGE   TOTAL DESTRUCTION ▓   WIDESPREAD DAMAGE ▒

DEPTFORD

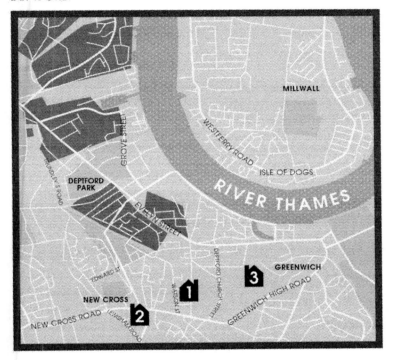

KEY TO INTERVIEWEES
1. **JEAN MUDDLE** WATSON STREET, SE8
2. **VIOLET HILLS** LEWISHAM WAY . SE8

KEY TO BOMB DAMAGE TOTAL DESTRUCTION ■ WIDESPREAD DAMAGE ▨

Links to additional resources

www.grandchildrenoftheblitz.com

An interactive website for the Grandchildren of the Blitz project containing all the interviews (in transcript and audio form), a photo gallery, a bomb damage map of the local area, a blog, information on all our young interviewers & interviewees and a timeline of events leading up to the Blitz

www.britishpathe.com/education

British Pathé is a film and newsreel archive, spanning from 1896 and 1976 which contains over 90,000 individual film items and 12 million stills, including Blitz footage. Schools can subscribe to the service and then access unlimited downloads of British Pathé material for use within the classroom

www.museumoflondon.org.uk/archive/exhibits/blitz/intro.html

An online exhibition which looks at what it was like to live through the Blitz in London and at how we remember it now. The exhibition collects memories from the Blitz – from experience and personal stories, TV, books, art, memorials and museums and brings them together in this exhibition

www.bbc.co.uk/ww2peopleswar/stories/41/a2613241.shtml

An archive of WW2 memories from those that lived through it, written by the public and gathered by the BBC. Included in this archive is 47,000 stories and 15,000 images

www.bbc.co.uk/schools/primaryhistory/world_war2/

An online resource for primary school children containing information about many aspects of WW2 including evacuation, air Raids, wartime homes and daily life and a resource area for teachers

aurora metro press

Founded in 1989 to publish and promote new writing, the
company has specialised in new drama and fiction, winning
recognition and awards from the industry.

drama

I HAVE BEFORE ME A REMARKABLE DOCUMENT
by Sonja Linden
ISBN 0-9546912-3-7 £7.99

HARVEST
by Manjula Padmanabhan
ISBN 0-9536757-7-7 £6.99

UNDER THE INFLUENCE
by Wayne Buchanan
ISBN 0-9536757-5-0 £7.99

TRASHED
by Noël Greig
ISBN 0-9546912-2-9 £7.99

LYSISTRATA - THE SEX STRIKE BY ARISTOPHANES
adapted by Germaine Greer and Phil Willmott
ISBN 0-9536757-0-8 £7.99

anthologies

SIX PLAYS BY BLACK AND ASIAN WOMEN WRITERS
ed. Kadija George
ISBN 0-9515877-2-2 £11.99

BLACK AND ASIAN PLAYS
introduced by Afia Nkrumah
ISBN 09536757-4-2 £9.95

SEVEN PLAYS BY WOMEN,
FEMALE VOICES, FIGHTING LIVES
ed. Cheryl Robson
ISBN 0-9515877-1-4 £5.95

A TOUCH OF THE DUTCH: PLAYS BY WOMEN
ed. Cheryl Robson
ISBN 0-9515877-7-3 £9.95

GRAEAE PLAYS 1:
NEW PLAYS REDEFINING DISABILITY
selected and introduced by Jenny Sealey
ISBN 0-9536757-6-9 £12.99

BEST OF THE FEST: NEW PLAYS CELEBRATING
10 YEARS OF LONDON NEW PLAY FESTIVAL
ed. Phil Setren
ISBN 0-9515877-8-1 £12.99

MEDITERRANEAN PLAYS BY WOMEN
ed. Marion Baraitser
ISBN 0-9515877-3-0 £9.95

EASTERN PROMISE, 7 PLAYS FROM CENTRAL
AND EASTERN EUROPE
eds. Sian Evans and Cheryl Robson
ISBN 0-9515877-9-X £11.99

anthologies of plays for young people:

THEATRE CENTRE: PLAYS FOR YOUNG PEOPLE
introduced by Rosamunde Hutt
ISBN 09542330-5-0 £12.99

CHARLES WAY: PLAYS FOR YOUNG PEOPLE
ISBN 0-9536757-1-8 £9.95

THE CLASSIC FAIRYTALES
retold for the stage by Charles Way
ISBN 0-9542330-0-X £11.50

ALL TALK, MONOLOGUES FOR YOUNG PEOPLE
ISBN 978-09551566-5-6 £7.99

new drama for young people

THE JUNGLE BOOK
by Rudyard Kilping
adapted by Neil Duffield
ISBN: 978-1906582265 £7.99

A CHRISTMAS CAROL
adapted by Neil Duffield
ISBN: 978-09551566-8-7 £8.99

TIN SOLDIER
by Noël Greig
ISBN: 978-19065821-9-7 £9.99

www.aurorametro.com